Contents

KU-513-049

This fluffy teddy
bear talks
quietly.

4

Finger painting

How does the paint feel on your hands?

messy

Cars and other vehicles

What noise does a car make?

BRRMMM BRRMMM

How do these vehicles sound?

NOISY

Clay modelling

You can make models out of clay.

What does it feel like when the clay squishes through your fingers?

messy

13

Cardboard models

You need lots of glue to stick a cardboard castle together.

messy

Glue sticks to lots of things, especially your hands!

15

Water wheels

You can get very wet when you play with a water wheel.

Do you wear a waterproof apron?

messy

Rattles and whistles

Rattles and whistles are really noisy!

NOISY

21

Touching and hearing

runny

dripping

23

Index

The end

Notes for adults

This series supports the young child's knowledge and understanding of their world. The following Early Learning Goals are relevant to the series.
• Find out about, and identify, some features of living things, objects and events that they observe.
• Exploration and investigation: feeling textures and materials.

The series explores a range of different play experiences by looking at features of different toys, the noises they make, or the noises children make when playing with them. The child is encouraged to think about what the noise indicates and whether the noises are loud or quiet. The toys in **Noisy Toys, Messy Toys** are made of a variety of materials including fabric, plastic, wood, metal and glass. 'Messy' play includes the use of other types of material: clay, water, paint and glue. It is important to note that the concepts of 'noisy' and 'messy' are not used in a negative sense but as a way of describing characteristics of toys.

There is an opportunity for the child to compare and contrast the different kinds of play as well as relating them to their own experiences, e.g. some children may find loud noises intimidating and others may dislike the feel of some of the messy activities. While reading the book, the child may enjoy making the noises suggested or go on to create their own noises. Similarly, they may be encouraged to try some of the messy activities shown in the book.

Follow-up activities
By making direct reference to the book the child can be encouraged to try new experiences, e.g. finding all their toys that make a noise. Drawing pictures and adding 'noise bubbles' would be an excellent way for the child to start making their own book.